This book ~~belongs to:~~ *is shared with*

_____

_____

_____

the boy who searched for silence

to all who sit

© 2016 Conscious Stories LLC

Illustrations by Alexis Aronson

Published by
Conscious Stories LLC

www.consciousstories.com

First Edition
ISBN 978-1-943750-00-9
Printed in China

1 2 3 4 5 6 7 8 9 10

Dear parents, teachers and readers

This story has been gift-wrapped with two simple mindfulness practices to help you connect more deeply with your children in the last 20 minutes of each day.

● Quietly set your intention for calm and open connection.

● Then start your story time with the **Snuggle Breathing Meditation**. Read each line aloud and take slow deep breaths together. This can be very relaxing and help everyone settle.

● At the end of the story you will find **The Gratitude Spiral**. This will help grow connection as you all share what you are thankful for.

Enjoy Snuggling into Togetherness!

Andrew

An easy breathing meditation

Snuggle Breathing

Our story begins with us breathing together.
Say each line aloud and then
take a slow deep breath in and out.

I breathe for me

I breathe for you

I breathe for us

I breathe for all that surrounds us

Once upon a time there was a boy
who went searching for silence.

He had heard that:

"Silence is golden"
    "Silence is peaceful"
        "Silence is blissful"

Most of all, he had heard that
in silence he could be himself.

He wanted nothing more.

This boy struggled with the
noise of everyday life.

There were cars and buses,
advertisements and programs,
instructions and advice.

Everywhere he went, noise entered in.
He found this very difficult,
so he went on a search for golden,
peaceful, blissful silence.

He walked to the bottom of the garden searching for silence, **but** the neighbor's dog was barking...

He walked to the park searching for silence, **but** the frisbee players were laughing...

He walked into the forest searching for silence, **but** the dog walkers were talking...

So he walked right up
to the top of the hill.

12

There he sighed,
"Aaah."

"I've done it,"
he thought as he
listened carefully.

"I've found silence."

BUT...

...just as he had the thought,
a noisy airplane flew over...

**VROOO
OOMMMMM!**

"Oh No!" he exclaimed.
"There is no silence out there in the world."

"This was a false quest," he thought.
"They lied to me," he blamed
"There is no such thing as golden,
peaceful, blissful silence."

"AAARGH!"

He raged with anger, stomping and shouting
and throwing rocks down the hill.

With time his anger softened.

"I will have to struggle with the difficult noises all my life."

"What am I to do?" he cried out loud.

He sat down.
Humpf
Utterly helpless,
he closed his
eyes and wept.

At first
he wept short,
breathless sobs,
gasping for each
new breath.

Over time his breathing
softened and deepened,
becoming deeper
and deeper.

'In....and...out'

The boy felt like he was falling...

...falling inwards.

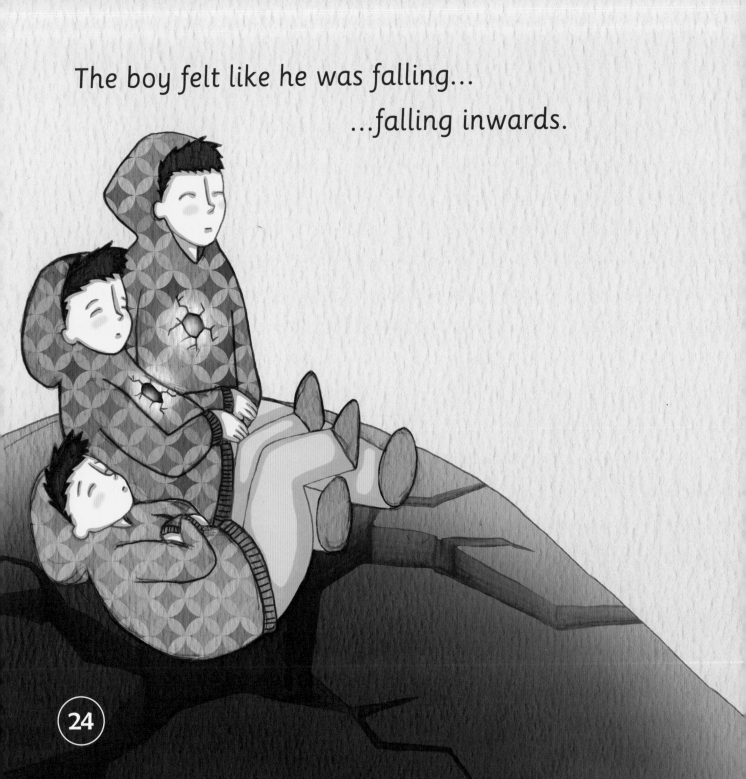

He was too tired
to be scared

... so he fell

He was too helpless
to think better

... so he fell

He was enjoying
the familiar feeling

... so he fell

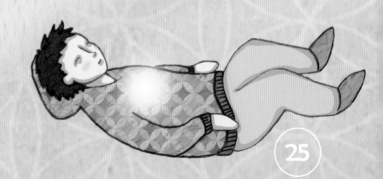

He fell

right

into

silence.

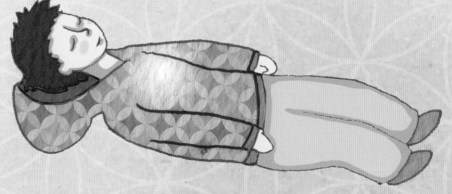

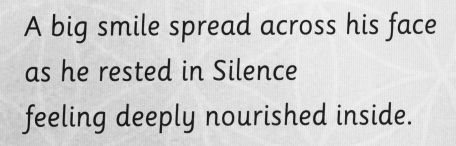

Silence was like a dream to him.
A whole world opened up.
It was spacious, comforting
and oh, so peaceful.

A big smile spread across his face
as he rested in Silence
feeling deeply nourished inside.

"AHA," he thought.

"Silence is not a thing to find –
it is a place inside me.

"I can go there and visit
whenever and wherever I want."

From inside silence he could hear another airplane fly overhead.

He simply smiled.

From inside silence he could hear the dog walkers talking.

He simply smiled.

From inside silence he could hear the frisbee players laughing,

and the boy simply smiled.

When he walked
down the hill,
    Silence came
with him...

When he walked
through the forest,
    Silence came
with him...

38

When he crossed
the park,
    Silence came
    with him...

Silence was
his friend.

That day he fell head-over-heels in love
with Silence.

He loved Silence so deeply
and Silence loved him back.

Each day after, he made sure to take twenty
special minutes to fall, inwards, into Silence.

All the things he had heard
turned out to be true.

He discovered that Silence is golden,
Silence is peaceful and
Silence is very deliciously blissful.

Most of all, he discovered that
in silence he could be himself.
This made him very, very happy.

What are you thankful for today?

Please read the questions in **The Gratitude Spiral** one at a time.

It is important that everyone gets to share (don't forget mom and dad!). This is a good moment to practice the balance between listening and sharing.

Reflect on your day
The Gratitude Spiral

1 What was your favourite part of the story?

2 What was your favourite part of your day?

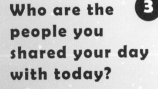

3 Who are the people you shared your day with today?

7 What do you need to tuck under your pillow tonight to help you tomorrow?

8 Do you need trust, love, kindness, courage, and friendship?

Who helped you with it? **6**

Sleep tight! Zzz **9**

4 What would you like to thank them for?

What one difficult thing happened today? **5**

the collection

The Conscious Bedtime Story Club

snuggling into togetherness

the prayer who searched for god
Coming Soon

the boy who searched for silence
Andrew Newman

the laughing witch
Andrew Newman

the fish who nearly drowned in his search for water

the elephant who tried to tiptoe

the dad who didn't know
Andrew Newman

the hug who got stuck

the forgetful elephant
Andrew Newman

a little light

the tree of goodness
Andrew Newman

the circle people
Coming Soon
Andrew Newman

the bee who could not choose a flower
Andrew Newman

what the club offers

A collection of stories with wise and lovable characters who teach spiritual values to your children

Delivered straight to your home over the course of one year.

One whole year of bedtime stories

Meet wonderful heroic characters with big hearts and deep values as they encounter exciting challenges and move towards freedom.

Simple mindfulness practices

Enjoy easy breathing practices that soften the atmosphere and create deep connection when reading together.

Create your own story books

Unleash your creativity by writing and coloring your own stories.

Reflective activity pages

Open sharing time with your children at the end of each day.

Delivered to your home

Make one decision today and experience a whole year of delightful stories.

Supportive parenting community

Join a community of conscious parents who seek connection with their children.

www.consciousstories.com

Andrew Newman – author

Andrew Newman has followed his deep longing for connection and his passion for spiritual development in a 12-year-long study of healing. He is a graduate of the Barbara Brennan School of Healing and a qualified Non-dual Kabbalistic healer. He has been actively involved in men's work through the Mankind Project since 2006.

His portfolio of work alongside his therapy practice includes publishing over 1500 donated poems as the PoemCatcher, volunteer coordination for Habitat for Humanity in South Africa and directing Edinburgh's Festival of Spirituality and Peace.

Alexis Aronson – illustrator

Alexis is a self taught illustrator, designer and artist, currently working from Cape Town, South Africa. She has a passion for serving projects with a visionary twist that incorporate image making with the growth of human consciousness for broader impact. Her media range from digital illustration and design to fine art techniques such as intaglio printmaking, ceramic sculpture and painting. In between working for clients and creating her own art for exhibition, Alexis is an avid nature lover, swimmer, yogi, hiker and gardener.

www.alexisaronson.com

I fall into silence.
I fall into silence.
I fall into silence.
I fall into silence.

I fall into silence.
I fall into silence.
I fall into silence.
I fall into silence.

I fall into silence.
I fall into silence.
I fall into silence.
I fall into silence.

The Conscious Bedtime Story Club
snuggling into togetherness

**stickers
for
sharing**

and for your
Star Counter

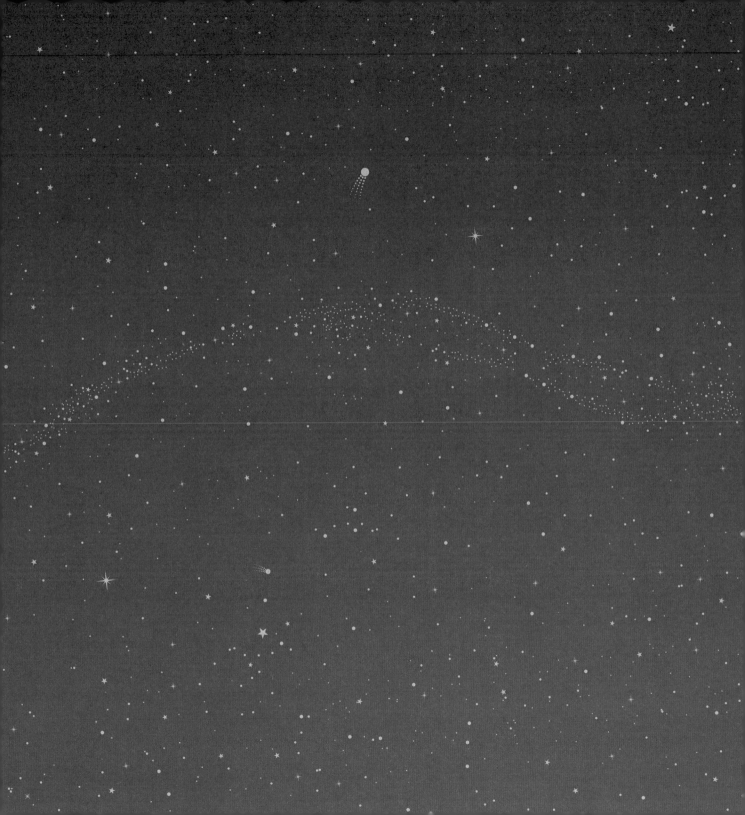

Star Counter

Every time you breathe together and
read aloud, you make a star shine in the
night sky.

Place a sticker, or color in a star, to count
how many times you have read this book.